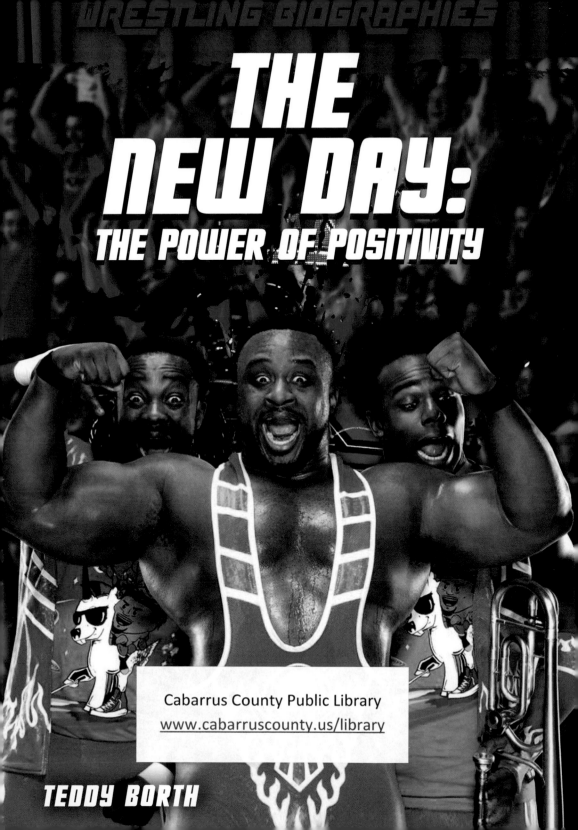

THE NEW DAY:
THE POWER OF POSITIVITY

TEDDY BORTH

abdopublishing.com

Published by Abdo Zoom, a division of ABDO, PO Box 398166, Minneapolis,
Minnesota 55439. Copyright © 2018 by Abdo Consulting Group, Inc. International
copyrights reserved in all countries. No part of this book may be reproduced in any form
without written permission from the publisher. Bolt!™ is a trademark and logo of Abdo Zoom.

Printed in the United States of America, North Mankato, Minnesota.
092017
012018

Photo Credits: Alamy, AllWrestlingSuperstars.com, iStock, Getty Images,
      Shutterstock, ©Miguel Discart p6, p20 / CC BY-SA 2.0
Production Contributors: Kenny Abdo, Jennie Forsberg, Grace Hansen
Design Contributors: Dorothy Toth, Neil Klinepier

Publisher's Cataloging-in-Publication Data

Names: Borth, Teddy, author.
Title: The New Day: the power of positivity / by Teddy Borth.
Other titles: The power of positivity
Description: Minneapolis, Minnesota: Abdo Zoom, 2018. | Series: Wrestling
      biographies | Includes online resource and index.
Identifiers: LCCN 2017939295 | ISBN 9781532121104 (lib.bdg.) |
      ISBN 9781532122224 (ebook) | ISBN 9781532122781 (Read-to-Me ebook)
Subjects: LCSH: The New Day (Big E, Kofi Kingston, Xavier Woods)--Juvenile
      literature. | Wrestlers—Juvenile literature. | Biography--Juvenile literature.
Classification: DDC 796.812 [B]--dc23
LC record available at https://lccn.loc.gov/2017939295

TABLE OF CONTENTS

The New Day is a **stable** of three wrestlers. They hold the record for longest tag team champion reign in WWE. They defended their **title** for 483 days.

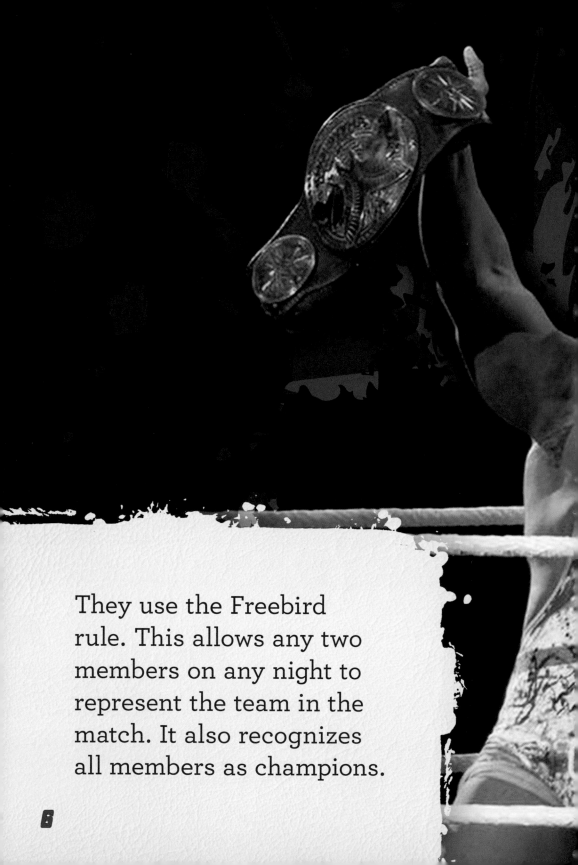

They use the Freebird
rule. This allows any two
members on any night to
represent the team in the
match. It also recognizes
all members as champions.

Kofi Kingston started
wrestling in 2006. He
has won many **singles**
championships in WWE.

Before wrestling, Big E was a United States **powerlifting** champion. He started in WWE **developmental** in 2009. He made his WWE TV debut in 2012.

Xavier Woods has been wrestling since 2005. After finding success in Georgia, Woods joined **TNA**. He then spent time in Japan. He signed with WWE in 2010.

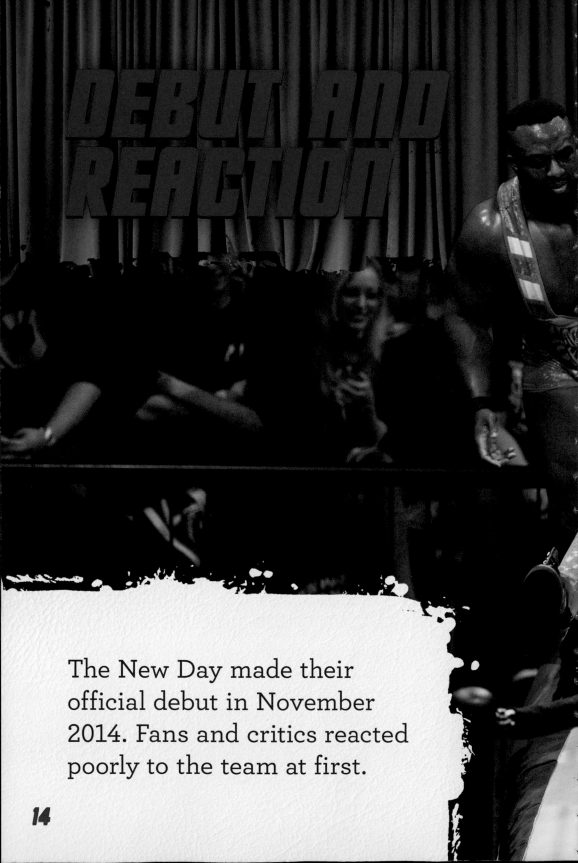

DEBUT AND REACTION

The New Day made their official debut in November 2014. Fans and critics reacted poorly to the team at first.

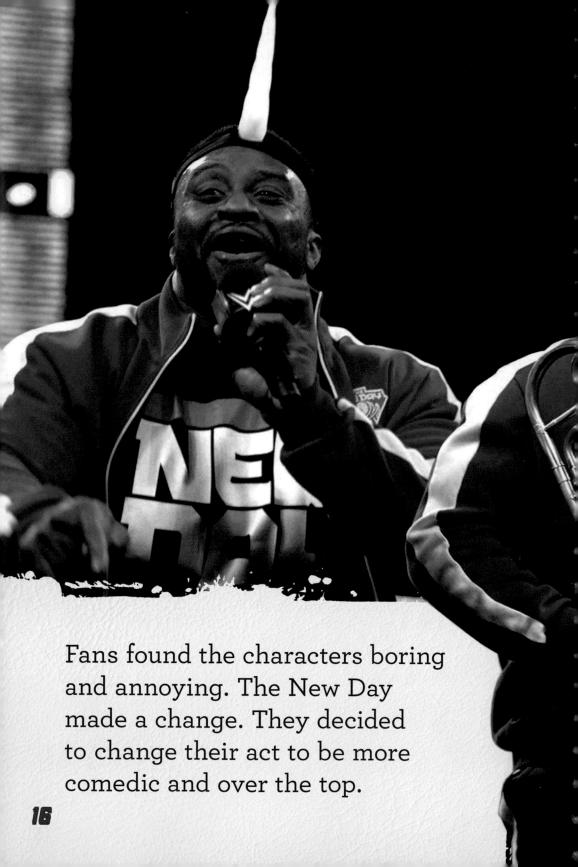

Fans found the characters boring
and annoying. The New Day
made a change. They decided
to change their act to be more
comedic and over the top.

They began making fun of
opponents. They introduced
trombones and unicorns into
their act. They became **villains**,
but the crowds loved it.

They had many great matches and funny **promos**. Fans started to chant for them. The New Day rose to be a top act in WWE.

GLOSSARY

developmental – a place where athletes can train and learn before going on TV.

powerlifting – a sport where competitors lift as much weight as they can.

promo – a promotional interview is when a wrestler talks on a microphone to either the crowd, interviewer, teammate or opponent. It is used to build a match up or advance a storyline.

singles – matches that are 1 versus 1.

stable – a group of wrestlers that have formed a unit.

title – championship; the position of being the best in a division.

Total Nonstop Action (TNA) – a wrestling company in the United States. In 2017, it changed to Global Force Wrestling.

villain – a person who is intentionally evil and cheats to win the match.

ONLINE RESOURCES

Booklinks
NONFICTION NETWORK
FREE! ONLINE NONFICTION RESOURCES

To learn more about The New Day, please
visit **abdobooklinks.com**. These links are
routinely monitored and updated to provide
the most current information available.

INDEX